COOKBOOK

THE EFFORTLESS CHEF SERIES

By
Chef Maggie Chow
Copyright © 2015 by Saxonberg
Associates
All rights reserved

Published by
BookSumo, a division of Saxonberg
Associates
http://www.booksumo.com/

Stay To the End of the Cookbook and Receive....

I really appreciate when people, take the time to read all of my recipes.

So, as a gift for reading this entire cookbook you will receive a **massive collection of special recipes.**

Read to the end of and get my *Easy Specialty Cookbook Box Set for FREE*!

This box set includes the following:

1. ***Easy Sushi Cookbook***
2. ***Easy Dump Dinner Cookbook***
3. ***Easy Beans Cookbook***

Remember this box set is about **EASY** cooking.

In the ***Easy Sushi Cookbook*** you will learn the easiest methods to prepare almost every type of Japanese Sushi i.e. *California Rolls, the Perfect Sushi Rice, Crab Rolls, Osaka Style Sushi*, and so many others.

Then we go on to *Dump Dinners*. Nothing can be easier than a Dump Dinner. In the ***Easy Dump Dinner Cookbook*** we will learn how to master our slow cookers and make some amazingly unique dinners that will take almost ***no effort***.

Finally in the ***Easy Beans Cookbook*** we tackle one of my favorite side dishes: Beans. There are so many delicious ways to make Baked Beans and Bean Salads that I had to share them.

So stay till the end and then keep on cooking with my *Easy Specialty Cookbook Box Set*!

ABOUT THE AUTHOR.

Maggie Chow is the author and creator of your favorite *Easy Cookbooks* and *The Effortless Chef Series*. Maggie is a lover of all things related to food. Maggie loves nothing more than finding new recipes, trying them out, and then making them her own, by adding or removing ingredients, tweaking cooking times, and anything to make the recipe not only taste better, but be easier to cook!

For a complete listing of all my books please see my author page.

INTRODUCTION

Welcome to *The Effortless Chef Series*! Thank you for taking the time to download the *Easy Greek Cookbook*. Come take a journey with me into the delights of easy cooking. The point of this cookbook and all my cookbooks is to exemplify the effortless nature of cooking simply.

In this book we focus on Greek cooking. You will find that even though the recipes are simple, the taste of the dishes is quite amazing.

So will you join me in an adventure of simple cooking? If the answer is yes (and I hope it is) please consult the table of contents to find the dishes you are most interested in. Once you are ready jump right in and start cooking.

— Chef Maggie Chow

TABLE OF CONTENTS

STAY TO THE END OF THE COOKBOOK AND RECEIVE............2

About the Author. 5

Introduction 7

Table of Contents 8

Any Issues? Contact Me 12

Legal Notes 13

Common Abbreviations 14

Chapter 1: Easy Greek Recipes 15

   Greek Style Baklava I 15

   Greek Moussaka I 19

   Soup of Carrots and Lentils 24

   Feta, Chicken, and Rosemary 27

   (Greek Style Kebabs) 27

   Maggie's Easy White Sauce 30

   (Tzatziki).......................................30

   Dolmas..33

   (Stuffed Grape Leaves) 33

Greek Style Shrimp 36
Sheftalia 39
(Tangy Greek Onions and Sausage) . 39
Classical Hummus I 42
Greek Style Salad Dressing 44
Pasta from Athens 47
Souvlaki II 50
Classical Hummus II 53
(Red) 53
Greek Style Macaroni Salad 56
Pita, Pesto, and Parmesan 59
(Greek Style Bake) 59
Mediterranean Pasta 62
Classical Hummus III 65
(Black Bean) 65
Greek Spinach Puff Pastry Bake 68
Souvlaki III 71
Penne Cannellini and Tomatoes Salad
.... 76
Easy Greek Style Chicken Breasts 79
Baked Greek Potatoes 82

Artisan Orzo from Greece 85
Greek Burgers 88
Chicken Soup 90
Bean Salad I 93
(Cucumbers, Garbanzos, and Olives) 93
Moussaka II 96
(Vegetarian Approved) 96
Greek Burgers II 101
Greek Rice 104
Easiest Greek Chicken 107
Parsley Pasta Salad 110
Orzo Salad II 113
Greek Falafel 116
Greek Puff Pastry Bake II 119
Souvlaki IV 122
Greek Style Minty Potato Bake 125
Easy Greek Dessert 128
Mediterranean Dijon Shrimp Salad 131
Greek Couscous 135

Greek Beans 138
Mediterranean Pork 140
Greek Party Dip 143
Easy Greek Penne and Steak 145
Rustic Potatoes with Oregano and Olives 148
Greek Honey Cake Dessert II 151
Veggie Salad 155
Greek Grilled Cheese 158
Avgolemono Chicken Stew 161
Souvlaki V 164
Shrimp with Feta and Tomatoes 168

THANKS FOR READING! NOW LET'S TRY SOME **SUSHI** AND **DUMP DINNERS** 171
Come On... 173
Let's Be Friends :) 173
Can I Ask A Favour? 174
Interested in Other Easy Cookbooks? 175

11

Any Issues? Contact Me

If you find that something important to you is missing from this book please contact me at maggie@booksumo.com.

I will try my best to re-publish a revised copy taking your feedback into consideration and let you know when the book has been revised with you in mind.

:)

— Chef Maggie Chow

LEGAL NOTES

ALL RIGHTS RESERVED. NO PART OF THIS BOOK MAY BE REPRODUCED OR TRANSMITTED IN ANY FORM OR BY ANY MEANS. PHOTOCOPYING, POSTING ONLINE, AND / OR DIGITAL COPYING IS STRICTLY PROHIBITED UNLESS WRITTEN PERMISSION IS GRANTED BY THE BOOK'S PUBLISHING COMPANY. LIMITED USE OF THE BOOK'S TEXT IS PERMITTED FOR USE IN REVIEWS WRITTEN FOR THE PUBLIC AND/OR PUBLIC DOMAIN.

COMMON ABBREVIATIONS

cup(s)	C.
tablespoon	tbsp
teaspoon	tsp
ounce	oz.
pound	lb

*All units used are standard American measurements

Chapter 1: Easy Greek Recipes

Greek Style Baklava I

Ingredients

- 8 oz. finely chopped pistachio nuts
- 8 oz. finely chopped hazelnuts
- 2 tsps ground cinnamon
- 1/2 tsp ground cloves
- 1/2 C. white sugar
- 2 C. unsalted butter, melted
- 1 1/2 (16 oz.) packages frozen phyllo pastry, thawed
- 1/4 C. whole cloves (optional)
- 3 C. white sugar
- 2 1/2 C. water
- 2 tbsps honey
- 1 tsp ground cinnamon
- 1/4 tsp ground cloves

Directions

- Get a jellyroll pan and coat it with butter then set your oven to 350 degrees before doing anything else.
- Get a bowl, combine: half a C. of sugar, pistachios, half a tsp of cloves, 2 tsps cinnamon, and hazelnuts.
- Now place a piece of pastry into the pan and coat it with some butter, add another layer, and more butter. Keep layering until have you have put 8 pieces on top of each other.
- Now add a layer of hazelnut mix. Put three more pieces of phyllo with butter in between. Then add more nuts. Keep going until you have no more hazelnut mix. Now finally add 8 more pieces of pastry and coat everything with more butter.
- Cut the layers into strips and then further cut everything into

triangles. Now add a clove to each one and then top the entire mix with butter.
- Cook the layers for 75 mins in the oven.
- At the same time get the following boiling: a quarter of a tsp of ground cloves, sugar (3 C.), 1 tsp cinnamon, honey, and water.
- Once everything is boiling set the heat to low and let the contents gently simmer for 20 mins.
- Shut the heat and let the mix cool.
- Top your baklava with the sauce. Now take out the cloves and discard them.
- Let everything cool before plating.
- Enjoy.

Amount per serving (60 total)

Timing Information:

Preparation	1 h
Cooking	1 h 25 m
Total Time	3 h 25 m

Nutritional Information:

Calories	182 kcal
Fat	10.9 g
Carbohydrates	20.1g
Protein	2.3 g
Cholesterol	16 mg
Sodium	72 mg

* Percent Daily Values are based on a 2,000 calorie diet.

Greek Moussaka I

Ingredients

- 3 eggplants, peeled and cut into 1/2 inch thick slices
- salt
- 1/4 C. olive oil
- 1 tbsp butter
- 1 lb. lean ground beef
- salt to taste
- ground black pepper to taste
- 2 onions, chopped
- 1 clove garlic, minced
- 1/4 tsp ground cinnamon
- 1/4 tsp ground nutmeg
- 1/2 tsp fines herbs
- 2 tbsps dried parsley
- 1 (8 oz.) can tomato sauce
- 1/2 C. red wine
- 1 egg, beaten
- 4 C. milk
- 1/2 C. butter
- 6 tbsps all-purpose flour

- salt to taste
- ground white pepper, to taste
- 1 1/2 C. freshly grated Parmesan cheese
- 1/4 tsp ground nutmeg

Directions

- On a working surface, layered with paper towels, lay out all your pieces of eggplant.
- Top the eggplants with salt and let them sit for 40 mins.
- Now sear the veggies in olive oil then place them on some new paper towels.
- Top your beef with pepper and salt and then fry it in butter with the garlic and onions.
- Once the beef is fully done add in: parsley, wine, cinnamon, tomato sauce, herbs, and nutmeg.
- Let this all cook for 23 mins.
- Let the mix cool off then add in the whisked eggs.

- Get a casserole dish and coat it with nonstick spray then set your oven to 350 degrees before doing anything else.
- Now get another pot and begin to heat your milk.
- In a separate pan mix flour and butter together until smooth and set the heat to low.
- Add in your milk slowly while stirring.
- Continue heating and stirring until everything is thick.
- Now add in the white pepper and some salt.
- Place most of your eggplant in the dish and top the eggplants with: the veggies, the meat, half of your parmesan, more eggplant, and the rest of the cheese.
- Cover everything with the milk sauce and then some nutmeg.
- Cook the layers for 60 mins in the oven.
- Then let the dish sit for 10 mins before serving.

- Enjoy.

Amount per serving (8 total)

Timing Information:

Preparation	45 m
Cooking	1 h
Total Time	1 h 45 m

Nutritional Information:

Calories	567 kcal
Fat	39.4 g
Carbohydrates	29.1g
Protein	23.6 g
Cholesterol	123 mg
Sodium	1017 mg

* Percent Daily Values are based on a 2,000 calorie diet.

SOUP OF CARROTS AND LENTILS

Ingredients

- 8 oz. brown lentils
- 1/4 C. olive oil
- 1 tbsp minced garlic
- 1 onion, minced
- 1 large carrot, chopped
- 1 quart water
- 1 pinch dried oregano
- 1 pinch crushed dried rosemary
- 2 bay leaves
- 1 tbsp tomato paste
- salt and ground black pepper to taste
- 1 tsp olive oil, or to taste
- 1 tsp red wine vinegar, or to taste (optional)

Directions

- Submerge your lentils, in water, in a big pot, and get it all boiling.

- Once it is boiling let the contents cook for 12 mins then remove all the liquids.
- Stir fry the carrots, onions, and garlic in olive oil for 7 mins then add in: bay leaves, lentils, rosemary, water (1 qt.), and oregano.
- Get everything boiling again, place a lid on the pot, and let the contents gently cook over a low level of heat for 12 mins.
- Now add in some pepper, salt, and your tomato paste.
- Place the lid back on the pot and cook everything for 35 more mins.
- Finally add in some olive oil and red wine vinegar before serving.
- Enjoy.

Amount per serving (4 total)

Timing Information:

Preparation	20 m
Cooking	1 h
Total Time	1 h 20 m

Nutritional Information:

Calories	357 kcal
Fat	15.5 g
Carbohydrates	40.3g
Protein	15.5 g
Cholesterol	0 mg
Sodium	57 mg

* Percent Daily Values are based on a 2,000 calorie diet.

Feta, Chicken, and Rosemary

(Greek Style Kebabs)

Ingredients

- 1 (8 oz.) container fat-free plain yogurt
- 1/3 C. crumbled feta cheese with basil and sun-dried tomatoes
- 1/2 tsp lemon zest
- 2 tbsps fresh lemon juice
- 2 tsps dried oregano
- 1/2 tsp salt
- 1/4 tsp ground black pepper
- 1/4 tsp crushed dried rosemary
- 1 lb. skinless, boneless chicken breast halves - cut into 1 inch pieces
- 1 large red onion, cut into wedges
- 1 large green bell pepper, cut into 1 1/2 inch pieces

Directions

- Get a bowl, combine: rosemary, yogurt, pepper, feta, salt, lemon zest, oregano, and lemon juice.
- Stir the contents until smooth then add in your chicken and stir everything again.
- Now place a covering of plastic around the bowl and putting everything in the fridge for 4 hrs.
- Get your grill hot and oil its grate.
- Stake your bell peppers, chicken, and onions onto skewers to form kebobs.
- Cook the kebobs on the grill until the chicken is fully done.
- Enjoy.

Amount per serving (4 total)

Timing Information:

Preparation	30 m
Cooking	15 m
Total Time	3 h 45 m

Nutritional Information:

Calories	243 kcal
Fat	7.5 g
Carbohydrates	12.3g
Protein	31 g
Cholesterol	85 mg
Sodium	632 mg

* Percent Daily Values are based on a 2,000 calorie diet.

Maggie's Easy White Sauce

(Tzatziki)

Ingredients

- 1 large English cucumber, peeled and grated
- 1/2 tsp salt
- 2 C. Greek yogurt
- 4 cloves garlic, minced
- 1 pinch cayenne pepper, or to taste
- 1/2 lemon, juiced
- 2 tbsps chopped fresh dill
- 1 tbsp chopped fresh mint
- salt and ground black pepper to taste
- 1 sprig fresh dill for garnish
- 1 pinch cayenne pepper for garnish

Directions

- Get a bowl, combine: cucumbers with half a tsp of salt.
- Let this sit for 15 mins.
- Now squeeze the cucumbers in some paper towel to get rid all of the liquids.
- Get a 2nd bowl for your yogurt and add in the squeezed cucumbers as well as: lemon, mint, black pepper, cayenne, salt, dill, and garlic.
- Place a covering of plastic around the bowl and put it all in the fridge for 5 hrs.
- Top the mix with some cayenne and more dill before serving.
- Enjoy with toasted pita.

Amount per serving (12 total)

Timing Information:

Preparation	
Cooking	15 m
Total Time	3 h 25 m

Nutritional Information:

Calories	49 kcal
Fat	3.4 g
Carbohydrates	2.5g
Protein	< 2.2 g
Cholesterol	8 mg
Sodium	120 mg

* Percent Daily Values are based on a 2,000 calorie diet.

Dolmas

(Stuffed Grape Leaves)

Ingredients

- 2 C. uncooked long-grain white rice
- 1 large onion, chopped
- 1/2 C. chopped fresh dill
- 1/2 C. chopped fresh mint leaves
- 2 quarts chicken broth
- 3/4 C. fresh lemon juice, divided
- 60 grape leaves, drained and rinsed
- hot water as needed
- 1 C. olive oil

Directions

- Stir fry the following for 7 mins: onions, rice, and dill.

- Now add in half of the broth and cook the mix for 17 mins with low level heat and a gentle boil.
- Add in half of the lemon juice and shut the heat.
- Layer 1 tsp of rice mix into the center of one grape leaf.
- Now roll this leaf into the shape of a burrito.
- Continue for all of your rice mix and then place all of the rolls into a big pot.
- Top everything in the pot with olive oil, broth, and lemon juice.
- Now place a lid on the pot and cook the mix for 65 mins with a low level of heat.
- You want to avoid boiling this mix.
- Shut the heat and let the rolls sit for 40 mins before layering them in a casserole dish to serve.
- Enjoy.

Amount per serving (12 total)

Timing Information:

Preparation	40 m
Cooking	1 h
Total Time	1 h 40 m

Nutritional Information:

Calories	303 kcal
Fat	18.7 g
Carbohydrates	30.9g
Protein	3.6 g
Cholesterol	0 mg
Sodium	573 mg

* Percent Daily Values are based on a 2,000 calorie diet.

Greek Style Shrimp

Ingredients

- 1 lb. medium shrimp, with shells
- 1 onion, chopped
- 2 tbsps chopped fresh parsley
- 1 C. white wine
- 1 (14.5 oz.) can diced tomatoes, drained
- 1/4 tsp garlic powder (optional)
- 1/4 C. olive oil
- 1 (8 oz.) package feta cheese, cubed
- salt and pepper to taste (optional)

Directions

- Submerge your shrimp in water and boil them for 7 mins, then drain all the liquids and place the shrimp in a bowl.
- Stir fry your onions in 2 tbsps of olive oil until tender and then

add: the rest of the olive oil, parsley, garlic powder, wine, and tomatoes.
- Cook this mix with a low heat and a gentle boil for 35 mins.
- At the same time remove the skins of the shrimp but leave the head and tails intact.
- After 35 mins of cooking the tomatoes, add in the shrimp, and cook for 7 more mins.
- Combine in the feta and shut the heat. Let the contents sit for 10 mins.
- Enjoy.

Amount per serving (4 total)

Timing Information:

Preparation	5 m
Cooking	35 m
Total Time	40 m

Nutritional Information:

Calories	441 kcal
Fat	26.6 g
Carbohydrates	10.1g
Protein	27.8 g
Cholesterol	223 mg
Sodium	1093 mg

* Percent Daily Values are based on a 2,000 calorie diet.

Sheftalia

(Tangy Greek Onions and Sausage)

Ingredients

- 1 lb. ground pork
- 1 large onion, finely chopped
- 1/2 C. finely chopped fresh parsley
- 1 pinch salt and pepper to taste
- 1 tbsp vinegar
- 1/2 lb. caul fat
- 10 skewers

Directions

- Get a bowl, combine: pepper, pork, salt, onions, and parsley.
- Get a 2nd bowl and add in vinegar and warm water.
- Add the caul to the water and leave it submerged for 3 mins.

- Now cut the caul into 4" rectangles.
- Add an equal amount of pork meat to each caul and then roll each one up.
- Continue until you have 10 sausages.
- Stake a skewer through each sausage and grill them for 22 mins.
- Flip each piece at least 4 times throughout the cooking time.
- Let the sausage cool before serving.
- Enjoy.

Amount per serving (3 total)

Timing Information:

Preparation	1 h
Cooking	1 h
Total Time	2 h

Nutritional Information:

Calories	1070 kcal
Fat	103.4 g
Carbohydrates	15.7g
Protein	27.7 g
Cholesterol	160 mg
Sodium	226 mg

* Percent Daily Values are based on a 2,000 calorie diet.

Classical Hummus I

Ingredients

- 2 C. canned garbanzo beans, drained
- 1/3 C. tahini
- 1/4 C. lemon juice
- 1 tsp salt
- 2 cloves garlic, halved
- 1 tbsp olive oil
- 1 pinch paprika
- 1 tsp minced fresh parsley

Directions

- Blend the following in a food processor until paste-like: garlic, garbanzos, salt, tahini, and lemon juice.
- Add this to a bowl with olive oil, paprika, and parsley.
- Enjoy.

Amount per serving (16 total)

Timing Information:

Preparation	
Cooking	10 m
Total Time	10 m

Nutritional Information:

Calories	77 kcal
Fat	4.3 g
Carbohydrates	8.1g
Protein	2.6 g
Cholesterol	0 mg
Sodium	236 mg

* Percent Daily Values are based on a 2,000 calorie diet.

Greek Style Salad Dressing

Ingredients

- 1 1/2 quarts olive oil
- 1/3 C. garlic powder
- 1/3 C. dried oregano
- 1/3 C. dried basil
- 1/4 C. pepper
- 1/4 C. salt
- 1/4 C. onion powder
- 1/4 C. Dijon-style mustard
- 2 quarts red wine vinegar

Directions

- Get bowl, combine: Dijon, olive oil, onion powder, garlic powder, salt, oregano, pepper, and basil.
- Now add in the vinegar and mix everything nicely.
- Place a covering over the bowl and serve the contents once all

the ingredients have reached room temp.
- Enjoy the dish over romaine lettuce and diced sun dried tomatoes.

Amount per serving (120 total)

Timing Information:

Preparation	
Cooking	10 m
Total Time	10 m

Nutritional Information:

Calories	104 kcal
Fat	10.8 g
Carbohydrates	2.1g
Protein	< 0.2 g
Cholesterol	< 0 mg
Sodium	246 mg

* Percent Daily Values are based on a 2,000 calorie diet.

Pasta from Athens

Ingredients

- 1 (16 oz.) package linguine pasta
- 1/2 C. chopped red onion
- 1 tbsp olive oil
- 2 cloves garlic, crushed
- 1 lb. skinless, boneless chicken breast meat - cut into bite-size pieces
- 1 (14 oz.) can marinated artichoke hearts, drained and chopped
- 1 large tomato, chopped
- 1/2 C. crumbled feta cheese
- 3 tbsps chopped fresh parsley
- 2 tbsps lemon juice
- 2 tsps dried oregano
- salt and pepper to taste
- 2 lemons, wedged, for garnish

Directions

- Cook your pasta in water and salt for 9 mins then remove all the liquids.
- Stir fry your garlic and onions in olive oil for 4 mins then add in the chicken and cook the mix until the chicken is fully done.
- Now set the heat to low and add the following: pasta, artichokes, oregano, tomato, lemon juice, feta, and parsley.
- Simmer this mix for 5 mins then shut the heat and add in pepper, salt, and lemon wedges.
- Enjoy.

Amount per serving (6 total)

Timing Information:

Preparation	15 m
Cooking	15 m
Total Time	30 m

Nutritional Information:

Calories	488 kcal
Fat	11.4 g
Carbohydrates	70g
Protein	32.6 g
Cholesterol	55 mg
Sodium	444 mg

* Percent Daily Values are based on a 2,000 calorie diet.

Souvlaki II

Ingredients

- 1 lemon, juiced
- 1/4 C. olive oil
- 1/4 C. soy sauce
- 1 tsp dried oregano
- 3 cloves garlic, crushed
- 4 lbs pork tenderloin, cut into 1 inch cubes
- 2 medium yellow onions, cut into 1 inch pieces
- 2 green bell peppers, cut into 1 inch pieces
- skewers

Directions

- Get a bowl, combine: green peppers, lemon juice, onions, olive oil, pork, soy sauce, garlic, and oregano.

- Place a covering on this mix and put it all in the fridge for 4 hrs.
- Now stake your pieces of onions, pork, and peppers onto skewers and grill them for 14 mins.
- Make sure you flip the kebabs multiple times while grilling.
- Enjoy.

Amount per serving (12 total)

Timing Information:

Preparation	30 m
Cooking	15 m
Total Time	2 h 45 m

Nutritional Information:

Calories	189 kcal
Fat	8.1 g
Carbohydrates	4.3g
Protein	24.2 g
Cholesterol	65 mg
Sodium	354 mg

* Percent Daily Values are based on a 2,000 calorie diet.

Classical Hummus II

(Red)

Ingredients

- 1 (15 oz.) can garbanzo beans, drained
- 1 (4 oz.) jar roasted red peppers
- 3 tbsps lemon juice
- 1 1/2 tbsps tahini
- 1 clove garlic, minced
- 1/2 tsp ground cumin
- 1/2 tsp cayenne pepper
- 1/4 tsp salt
- 1 tbsp chopped fresh parsley

Directions

- Blend the following until smooth: salt, chickpeas, cayenne, red peppers, cumin, lemon juice, garlic, and tahini.

- Add everything to a bowl and place a covering of plastic over it.
- Now place it all in the fridge for 60 mins.
- Before serving the mix top the hummus with parsley.
- Enjoy.

Amount per serving (8 total)

Timing Information:

Preparation	
Cooking	15 m
Total Time	1 h 15 m

Nutritional Information:

Calories	64 kcal
Fat	2.2 g
Carbohydrates	9.6g
Protein	2.5 g
Cholesterol	0 mg
Sodium	370 mg

* Percent Daily Values are based on a 2,000 calorie diet.

Greek Style Macaroni Salad

Ingredients

- 1/2 C. olive oil
- 1/2 C. red wine vinegar
- 1 1/2 tsps garlic powder
- 1 1/2 tsps dried basil
- 1 1/2 tsps dried oregano
- 3/4 tsp ground black pepper
- 3/4 tsp white sugar
- 2 1/2 C. cooked elbow macaroni
- 3 C. fresh sliced mushrooms
- 15 cherry tomatoes, halved
- 1 C. sliced red bell peppers
- 3/4 C. crumbled feta cheese
- 1/2 C. chopped green onions
- 1 (4 oz.) can whole black olives
- 3/4 C. sliced pepperoni sausage, cut into strips

Directions

- Get a bowl, combine: sugar, pepperoni, olive oil, olives, pasta, black pepper, onions, feta, mushrooms, red peppers, tomatoes, vinegar, oregano, garlic powder, and basil.
- Place a covering of plastic around the bowl and place everything in the fridge for 3 hrs.
- Enjoy.

Amount per serving (4 total)

Timing Information:

Preparation	15 m
Cooking	10 m
Total Time	2 h 25 m

Nutritional Information:

Calories	746 kcal
Fat	56.1 g
Carbohydrates	40.4g
Protein	22.1 g
Cholesterol	70 mg
Sodium	1279 mg

* Percent Daily Values are based on a 2,000 calorie diet.

Pita, Pesto, and Parmesan (Greek Style Bake)

Ingredients

- 1 (6 oz.) tub sun-dried tomato pesto
- 6 (6 inch) whole wheat pita breads
- 2 roma (plum) tomatoes, chopped
- 1 bunch spinach, rinsed and chopped
- 4 fresh mushrooms, sliced
- 1/2 C. crumbled feta cheese
- 2 tbsps grated Parmesan cheese
- 3 tbsps olive oil
- ground black pepper to taste

Directions

- Set your oven to 350 degrees before doing anything else.

- Coat each piece of pita with some pesto and then layer each with: pepper, tomatoes, olive oil, spinach, parmesan, mushrooms, and feta.
- Cook the bread, for 15 mins, in the oven, and then cut them into triangles before serving.
- Enjoy.

Amount per serving (6 total)

Timing Information:

Preparation	10 m
Cooking	12 m
Total Time	22 m

Nutritional Information:

Calories	350 kcal
Fat	17.1 g
Carbohydrates	41.6g
Protein	11.6 g
Cholesterol	13 mg
Sodium	587 mg

* Percent Daily Values are based on a 2,000 calorie diet.

Mediterranean Pasta

Ingredients

- 1 (16 oz.) package penne pasta
- 1 1/2 tbsps butter
- 1/2 C. chopped red onion
- 2 cloves garlic, minced
- 1 lb. skinless, boneless chicken breast halves - cut into bite-size pieces
- 1 (14 oz.) can artichoke hearts in water
- 1 tomato, chopped
- 1/2 C. crumbled feta cheese
- 3 tbsps chopped fresh parsley
- 2 tbsps lemon juice
- 1 tsp dried oregano
- salt to taste
- ground black pepper to taste

Directions

- Boil your pasta in water and salt for 9 mins then remove all the liquids.
- At the same time, stir fry your garlic and onions in butter for 4 mins, then combine in the chicken, and cook everything for 9 more mins.
- Set the heat to a low level and add in your artichokes after chopping them and discarding their liquids.
- Cook this mix for 3 more mins before adding in: pasta, tomatoes, oregano, feta, lemon juice, and the fresh parsley.
- Cook everything for 4 mins to get it all hot. Then add in your pepper and salt after shutting the heat.
- Enjoy.

Amount per serving (4 total)

Timing Information:

Preparation	20 m
Cooking	30 m
Total Time	50 m

Nutritional Information:

Calories	685 kcal
Fat	13.2 g
Carbohydrates	96.2g
Protein	47 g
Cholesterol	94 mg
Sodium	826 mg

* Percent Daily Values are based on a 2,000 calorie diet.

Classical Hummus III

(Black Bean)

Ingredients

- 1 clove garlic
- 1 (15 oz.) can black beans; drain and reserve liquid
- 2 tbsps lemon juice
- 1 1/2 tbsps tahini
- 3/4 tsp ground cumin
- 1/2 tsp salt
- 1/4 tsp cayenne pepper
- 1/4 tsp paprika
- 10 Greek olives

Directions

- Blend your garlic in a blender with a few pulses to mince it then add in: half of your cayenne, black beans, salt, 2 tbsps of black

bean juice, half tsp cumin, tahini, and lemon juice.
- Blend this mix until it has the consistency of hummus.
- Add everything to a bowl and top it all with olives and paprika.
- Enjoy.

Amount per serving (8 total)

Timing Information:

Preparation	
Cooking	5 m
Total Time	5 m

Nutritional Information:

Calories	81 kcal
Fat	3.1 g
Carbohydrates	10.3g
Protein	3.9 g
Cholesterol	0 mg
Sodium	427 mg

* Percent Daily Values are based on a 2,000 calorie diet.

Greek Spinach Puff Pastry Bake

Ingredients

- 3 tbsps olive oil
- 1 large onion, chopped
- 1 bunch green onions, chopped
- 2 cloves garlic, minced
- 2 lbs spinach, rinsed and chopped
- 1/2 C. chopped fresh parsley
- 2 eggs, lightly beaten
- 1/2 C. ricotta cheese
- 1 C. crumbled feta cheese
- 8 sheets phyllo dough
- 1/4 C. olive oil

Directions

- Coat a baking pan with nonstick spray and then set your oven to 350 degrees before doing anything else.

- Stir fry your garlic, onions, and green onions in olive oil for 4 mins. Then add in, the parsley and the spinach, and cook it all for 3 more mins.
- Remove all the contents.
- Get a bowl, combine: feta, onion mix, ricotta, and eggs.
- Coat a piece of phyllo with olive oil then layer it in the pan.
- Add another piece and also more olive oil.
- Do this two more times.
- Add your ricotta mix and fold the phyllo around the filling and seal it.
- Cook everything in the oven for 35 mins.
- Then cut the contents into your preferred shape.
- Enjoy.

Amount per serving (5 total)

Timing Information:

Preparation	30 m
Cooking	1 h
Total Time	1 h 30 m

Nutritional Information:

Calories	528 kcal
Fat	36.7 g
Carbohydrates	32.8g
Protein	21 g
Cholesterol	108 mg
Sodium	925 mg

* Percent Daily Values are based on a 2,000 calorie diet.

Souvlaki III

Ingredients

Marinade:

- 3/4 C. balsamic vinaigrette salad dressing
- 3 tbsps lemon juice
- 1 tbsp dried oregano
- 1/2 tsp freshly ground black pepper
- 4 skinless, boneless chicken breast halves

White Sauce:

- 1/2 C. seeded, shredded cucumber
- 1 tsp kosher salt
- 1 C. plain yogurt
- 1/4 C. sour cream
- 1 tbsp lemon juice

- 1/2 tbsp rice vinegar
- 1 tsp olive oil
- 1 clove garlic, minced
- 1 tbsp chopped fresh dill
- 1/2 tsp Greek seasoning
- kosher salt to taste
- freshly ground black pepper to taste
- 4 large pita bread rounds
- 1 heart of romaine lettuce, cut into 1/4 inch slices
- 1 red onion, thinly sliced
- 1 tomato, halved and sliced
- 1/2 C. kalamata olives
- 1/2 C. pepperoncini
- 1 C. crumbled feta cheese

Directions

- Get a bowl, combine: chicken, black pepper (1/2 tsp), balsamic, oregano, and the juice of half of a lemon.

- Place a covering on the bowl and place the contents in the fridge for 2 hrs.
- Get a 2nd bowl and add in your cucumbers after shredding them and also some kosher salt.
- Let this stand for 10 mins.
- Get a 3rd bowl, combine: olive oil, garlic, yogurt, dill, rice vinegar, Greek seasoning, sour cream, and 1 tbsp of lemon juice.
- Place this mix in the fridge.
- Now grill your chicken pieces for 9 mins then flip them and cook the chicken pieces for 9 more mins.
- Let the chicken cool and then julienne it.
- Grill your pieces of pita for 3 mins and flip them throughout the entire grilling time.
- Fill each piece of pita with: pepperoncini, chicken, olive, lettuce, tomato, and onions.
- Add a topping of white sauce from the fridge and some feta on the side.

- Enjoy.

Amount per serving (4 total)

Timing Information:

Preparation	30 m
Cooking	20 m
Total Time	1 h 50 m

Nutritional Information:

Calories	764 kcal
Fat	40.5 g
Carbohydrates	55.9g
Protein	44.4 g
Cholesterol	133 mg
Sodium	3170 mg

* Percent Daily Values are based on a 2,000 calorie diet.

Penne Cannellini and Tomatoes Salad

Ingredients

- 2 (14.5 oz.) cans Italian-style diced tomatoes
- 1 (19 oz.) can cannellini beans, drained and rinsed
- 10 oz. fresh spinach, washed and chopped
- 8 oz. penne pasta
- 1/2 C. crumbled feta cheese

Directions

- Boil your pasta in water and salt for 9 mins then remove the liquids.
- At the same time get the following boiling: beans and tomatoes.
- Cook the mix for 13 mins with a low level of heat.

- Now combine in the spinach and cook everything for 4 more mins.
- Top the pasta with the sauce and cheese.
- Enjoy.

Amount per serving (4 total)

Timing Information:

Preparation	10 m
Cooking	15 m
Total Time	25 m

Nutritional Information:

Calories	460 kcal
Fat	5.9 g
Carbohydrates	79g
Protein	23.4 g
Cholesterol	17 mg
Sodium	593 mg

* Percent Daily Values are based on a 2,000 calorie diet.

Easy Greek Style Chicken Breasts

Ingredients

- 2 tbsps all-purpose flour, divided
- 1/2 tsp salt
- 1/4 tsp black pepper
- 1/4 lb. feta cheese, crumbled
- 1 tbsp fresh lemon juice
- 1 tsp dried oregano
- 6 boneless, skinless chicken breast halves, flatten to 1/2 thickness
- 2 tbsps olive oil
- 1 1/2 C. water
- 1 cube chicken bouillon, crumbled
- 2 C. loosely packed torn fresh spinach leaves
- 1 ripe tomato, chopped

Directions

- Get a bowl, mix: oregano, cheese, and lemon juice.
- Get a 2nd bowl, combine: bouillon, 1 C. of water, and flour.
- Dredge you chicken in a mix of pepper, salt, and flour.
- Then fold each piece and stake a toothpick through each one.
- Sear the chicken in oil for 3 mins per side. Then top the chicken with the contents of the 2nd bowl.
- Cook everything for 1 more min before adding tomatoes and spinach.
- Get everything boiling and then place a lid on the pot.
- Set the heat to low and let it all cook for 12 mins.
- Enjoy.

Amount per serving (6 total)

Timing Information:

Preparation	20 m
Cooking	20 m
Total Time	40 m

Nutritional Information:

Calories	239 kcal
Fat	10.2 g
Carbohydrates	4.8g
Protein	31 g
Cholesterol	85 mg
Sodium	686 mg

* Percent Daily Values are based on a 2,000 calorie diet.

Baked Greek Potatoes

Ingredients

- 1/3 C. olive oil
- 1 1/2 C. water
- 2 cloves garlic, finely chopped
- 1/4 C. fresh lemon juice
- 1 tsp dried thyme
- 1 tsp dried rosemary
- 2 cubes chicken bouillon
- ground black pepper to taste
- 6 potatoes, peeled and quartered

Directions

- Set your oven to 350 degrees before doing anything else.
- Get a bowl, combine: pepper, olive oil, bouillon, water, rosemary, water, thyme, garlic, and lemon juice.

- Layer the potatoes in a casserole dish and top everything with the lemon mix.
- Place some foil around the dish and cook the contents in the oven for 90 mins.
- Flip the potatoes every 30 mins while cooking.
- Enjoy.

Amount per serving (4 total)

Timing Information:

Preparation	20 m
Cooking	2 h
Total Time	2 h 20 m

Nutritional Information:

Calories	418 kcal
Fat	18.5 g
Carbohydrates	58.6g
Protein	7 g
Cholesterol	< 1 mg
Sodium	< 596 mg

* Percent Daily Values are based on a 2,000 calorie diet.

Artisan Orzo from Greece

Ingredients

- 1 1/2 C. uncooked orzo pasta
- 2 (6 oz.) cans marinated artichoke hearts, drained, liquid reserved
- 1 tomato, seeded and chopped
- 1 cucumber, seeded and chopped
- 1 red onion, chopped
- 1 C. crumbled feta cheese
- 1 (2 oz.) can black olives, drained
- 1/4 C. chopped fresh parsley
- 1 tbsp lemon juice
- 1/2 tsp dried oregano
- 1/2 tsp lemon pepper

Directions

- Boil your pasta in water and salt for 9 mins then remove all the liquids.

- Get a bowl, mix: lemon pepper, artichokes, oregano, lemon juice, tomatoes, pasta, parsley, cucumbers, olives, feta, and onions.
- Stir the contents, place a covering on the bowl, and put everything in the fridge for 2 hrs.
- Top the salad with the artichoke liquid and serve.
- Enjoy.

Amount per serving (6 total)

Timing Information:

Preparation	1 h 10 m
Cooking	10 m
Total Time	1 h 20 m

Nutritional Information:

Calories	348 kcal
Fat	10.2 g
Carbohydrates	53.2g
Protein	13.9 g
Cholesterol	22 mg
Sodium	615 mg

* Percent Daily Values are based on a 2,000 calorie diet.

Greek Burgers

Ingredients

- 1 lb. ground turkey
- 1 C. crumbled feta cheese
- 1/2 C. kalamata olives, pitted and sliced
- 2 tsps dried oregano
- ground black pepper to taste

Directions

- Get a bowl, combine: pepper, turkey, oregano, feta, and olives. Shape this into burgers and then grill each one for 6 mins.
- Flip the patty and cook it for 7 more mins.
- Enjoy.

Amount per serving (4 total)

Timing Information:

Preparation	10 m
Cooking	20 m
Total Time	40 m

Nutritional Information:

Calories	318 kcal
Fat	21.9 g
Carbohydrates	3.6g
Protein	25.5 g
Cholesterol	123 mg
Sodium	800 mg

* Percent Daily Values are based on a 2,000 calorie diet.

Chicken Soup

Ingredients

- 8 C. chicken broth
- 1/2 C. fresh lemon juice
- 1/2 C. shredded carrots
- 1/2 C. chopped onion
- 1/2 C. chopped celery
- 6 tbsps chicken soup base
- 1/4 tsp ground white pepper
- 1/4 C. margarine
- 1/4 C. all-purpose flour
- 1 C. cooked white rice
- 1 C. diced, cooked chicken meat
- 16 slices lemon
- 8 egg yolks

Directions

- Get the following boiling: white pepper, chicken broth, soup base, celery, lemon juice, onions, and carrots.

- Set the heat to low and let the contents cook for 23 mins.
- Begin heating the flour and butter while stirring and then add in the soup while continuing to stir and cook the mix for 12 more mins.
- Now start whisking your eggs and then add in some soup while continuing to whisk.
- Add the entire mix to your soup and also add the chicken and the rice.
- When serving the soup top it with some pieces of lemon.
- Enjoy.

Amount per serving (16 total)

Timing Information:

Preparation	25 m
Cooking	40 m
Total Time	1 h 5 m

Nutritional Information:

Calories	124 kcal
Fat	6.6 g
Carbohydrates	9.1g
Protein	7.8 g
Cholesterol	110 mg
Sodium	1237 mg

* Percent Daily Values are based on a 2,000 calorie diet.

Bean Salad I

(Cucumbers, Garbanzos, and Olives)

Ingredients

- 2 (15 oz.) cans garbanzo beans, drained
- 2 cucumbers, halved lengthwise and sliced
- 12 cherry tomatoes, halved
- 1/2 red onion, chopped
- 2 cloves garlic, minced
- 1 (15 oz.) can black olives, drained and chopped
- 1 oz. crumbled feta cheese
- 1/2 C. Italian-style salad dressing
- 1/2 lemon, juiced
- 1/2 tsp garlic salt
- 1/2 tsp ground black pepper

Directions

- Get a bowl, toss: pepper, beans, garlic salt, cucumbers, lemon juice, tomatoes, dressing, onions, cheese, garlic, and olives.
- Place a covering on the bowl and put everything in the fridge for 3 hrs.
- Enjoy.

Amount per serving (8 total)

Timing Information:

Preparation	
Cooking	10 m
Total Time	2 h 10 m

Nutritional Information:

Calories	214 kcal
Fat	11.5 g
Carbohydrates	25.5g
Protein	5.2 g
Cholesterol	3 mg
Sodium	1067 mg

* Percent Daily Values are based on a 2,000 calorie diet.

Moussaka II

(Vegetarian Approved)

Ingredients

- 1 eggplant, thinly sliced
- 1 tbsp olive oil, or more as needed
- 1 large zucchini, thinly sliced
- 2 potatoes, thinly sliced
- 1 onion, sliced
- 1 clove garlic, chopped
- 1 tbsp white vinegar
- 1 (14.5 oz.) can whole peeled tomatoes, chopped
- 1/2 (14.5 oz.) can lentils, drained with liquid reserved
- 1 tsp dried oregano
- 2 tbsps chopped fresh parsley
- salt and ground black pepper to taste
- 1 C. crumbled feta cheese
- 1 1/2 tbsps butter
- 2 tbsps all-purpose flour
- 1 1/4 C. milk

- ground black pepper to taste
- 1 pinch ground nutmeg
- 1 egg, beaten
- 1/4 C. grated Parmesan cheese

Directions

- Get a bowl and add in your eggplants. Coat them with salt and let them sit for 40 mins.
- Now drain the resulting liquids and dry the eggplants with some paper towel.
- Set your oven to 375 degrees before doing anything else.
- Sear your zucchini and eggplants in oil for 4 mins per side. Then place the zucchini to the side on some paper towels.
- Now begin to stir fry your potatoes in the same pot for 6 mins then flip them and cook it all for 6 more mins. Place these to the side as well.
- Add in some more oil if needed and then start to stir fry your

garlic and onions for 8 mins. Add the vinegar and get everything boiling.
- Once it is all boiling, set the heat to low, and cook the mix until everything is thick.
- Now add in: parsley, tomatoes, oregano, lentils, and half of the lentil juice.
- Place a lid on the pot and cook the contents for 17 mins with the same level of low heat.
- Get a casserole dish and add in 1/3 of the zucchini then the same amount of eggplant, then half of the following on top: feta, onions, and potatoes.
- Top everything with the tomato mix and then continue the layering.
- Once all of the ingredients have been used. Cooked the dish in the oven for 30 mins.
- Get the following boiling: milk, butter, and flour.

- Stir the contents as it begins to boil and once the mix is sauce like add in the nutmeg and pepper.
- Let the contents cool a bit then add in whisked eggs.
- Top the casserole with the egg mix and some parmesan and cook everything for 30 more mins.
- Enjoy.

Amount per serving (7 total)

Timing Information:

Preparation	30 m
Cooking	1 h 30 m
Total Time	2 h

Nutritional Information:

Calories	240 kcal
Fat	11.8 g
Carbohydrates	25.5g
Protein	10.2 g
Cholesterol	58 mg
Sodium	426 mg

* Percent Daily Values are based on a 2,000 calorie diet.

Greek Burgers II

Ingredients

- 1/2 lb. lean ground beef
- 1/2 lb. lean ground lamb
- 1/2 onion, grated
- 2 cloves garlic, pressed
- 1 slice bread, toasted and crumbled
- 1/2 tsp dried savory
- 1/2 tsp ground allspice
- 1/2 tsp ground coriander
- 1/2 tsp salt
- 1/2 tsp ground black pepper
- 1 dash ground cumin

Directions

- Get a bowl, mix: bread crumbs, cumin, savory, pepper, allspice, beef, onions, salt, coriander, and lamb.

- Mix the meats and spice with your hands until firm and then form the mix into 4 burgers.
- Grill these burgers for 8 mins per side.
- Enjoy.

Amount per serving (4 total)

Timing Information:

Preparation	10 m
Cooking	15 m
Total Time	25 m

Nutritional Information:

Calories	338 kcal
Fat	25.4 g
Carbohydrates	5.7g
Protein	20.3 g
Cholesterol	84 mg
Sodium	408 mg

* Percent Daily Values are based on a 2,000 calorie diet.

GREEK RICE

Ingredients

- 1/3 C. olive oil
- 2 onions, chopped
- 2 lbs fresh spinach, rinsed and stemmed
- 1 (8 oz.) can tomato sauce
- 2 C. water
- 1 tsp dried dill weed
- 1 tsp dried parsley
- salt and pepper to taste
- 1/2 C. uncooked white rice

Directions

- Stir fry your onions in olive oil until see-through then add in: spinach, water, and tomato sauce.
- Get everything boiling and then add: pepper, parsley, salt, and dill.

- Cook the mix for 2 mins while boiling then add the rice.
- Set the heat to low and cook everything for 27 mins.
- Enjoy.

Amount per serving (4 total)

Timing Information:

Preparation	5 m
Cooking	45 m
Total Time	50 m

Nutritional Information:

Calories	337 kcal
Fat	19.3 g
Carbohydrates	35.7g
Protein	9.8 g
Cholesterol	0 mg
Sodium	553 mg

* Percent Daily Values are based on a 2,000 calorie diet.

Easiest Greek Chicken

Ingredients

- 4 skinless, boneless chicken breast halves
- 1 C. extra virgin olive oil
- 1 lemon, juiced
- 2 tsps crushed garlic
- 1 tsp salt
- 1 1/2 tsps black pepper
- 1/3 tsp paprika

Directions

- Slice a few incisions into your pieces of chicken before doing anything else.
- Now get a bowl, combine: paprika, olive oil, pepper, lemon juice, salt, and garlic.
- Now add in the chicken and place the contents in the fridge for 8 hrs.

- Grill your chicken until fully done with indirect heat on the side of the grill with the grilling grates oiled.
- Enjoy.

Amount per serving (4 total)

Timing Information:

Preparation	10 m
Cooking	8 h
Total Time	8 h 30 m

Nutritional Information:

Calories	644 kcal
Fat	57.6 g
Carbohydrates	4g
Protein	27.8 g
Cholesterol	68 mg
Sodium	660 mg

* Percent Daily Values are based on a 2,000 calorie diet.

Parsley Pasta Salad

Ingredients

- 2 (9 oz.) packages cheese tortellini
- 1/2 C. extra virgin olive oil
- 1/4 C. lemon juice
- 1/4 C. red wine vinegar
- 2 tbsps chopped fresh parsley
- 1 tsp dried oregano
- 1/2 tsp salt
- 6 eggs
- 1 lb. baby spinach leaves
- 1 C. crumbled feta cheese
- 1/2 C. slivered red onion

Directions

- Boil your pasta in water and salt for 9 mins then remove all the liquids.

- Get a bowl, mix: salt, olive oil, oregano, lemon juice, pasta, parsley, and vinegar.
- Stir the contents and then place everything in the fridge for 3 hrs.
- Get your eggs boiling in water, place a lid on the pot, and shut the heat.
- Let the eggs stand for 15 mins. Then peel, and cut them into quarters.
- Take out the bowl in the fridge and add in: onions, eggs, feta, and spinach.
- Stir everything before serving.
- Enjoy.

Amount per serving (8 total)

Timing Information:

Preparation	15 m
Cooking	15 m
Total Time	2 h 30 m

Nutritional Information:

Calories	486 kcal
Fat	30.3 g
Carbohydrates	35.7g
Protein	19.8 g
Cholesterol	196 mg
Sodium	836 mg

* Percent Daily Values are based on a 2,000 calorie diet.

Orzo Salad II

Ingredients

- 1 C. uncooked orzo pasta
- 1/4 C. pitted green olives
- 1 C. diced feta cheese
- 3 tbsps chopped fresh parsley
- 3 tbsps chopped fresh dill
- 1 ripe tomato, chopped
- 1/4 C. virgin olive oil
- 1/8 C. lemon juice
- salt and pepper to taste

Directions

- Cook your orzo in boiling water with salt for 9 mins.
- Then remove the liquid and run the pasta under cool water.
- Now get a bowl, combine: tomato, olive, dill, feta, parsley, and orzo.

- Get a 2nd bowl, mix: lemon juice pepper, salt, and oil.
- Combine both bowls and toss everything.
- Place the mix in the fridge until cold.
- Enjoy.

Amount per serving (6 total)

Timing Information:

Preparation	15 m
Cooking	10 m
Total Time	25 m

Nutritional Information:

Calories	329 kcal
Fat	19.6 g
Carbohydrates	28.1g
Protein	10.9 g
Cholesterol	37 mg
Sodium	614 mg

* Percent Daily Values are based on a 2,000 calorie diet.

Greek Falafel

Ingredients

- 1 (19 oz.) can garbanzo beans, rinsed and drained
- 1 small onion, finely chopped
- 2 cloves garlic, minced
- 1 1/2 tbsps chopped fresh cilantro
- 1 tsp dried parsley
- 2 tsps ground cumin
- 1/8 tsp ground turmeric
- 1/2 tsp baking powder
- 1 C. fine dry bread crumbs
- 3/4 tsp salt
- 1/4 tsp cracked black peppercorns
- 1 quart vegetable oil for frying

Directions

- Get a bowl, combine: pepper, onions, salt, garlic, bread crumbs, cilantro, baking powder, parsley,

mashed garbanzos, turmeric, and cumin.
- Form the contents into small balls and make about 20 of them.
- Deep fry these falafels in hot oil until golden.
- Enjoy.

Amount per serving (6 total)

Timing Information:

Preparation	25 m
Cooking	7 m
Total Time	32 m

Nutritional Information:

Calories	317 kcal
Fat	16.8 g
Carbohydrates	35.2g
Protein	7.2 g
Cholesterol	0 mg
Sodium	724 mg

* Percent Daily Values are based on a 2,000 calorie diet.

Greek Puff Pastry Bake II

Ingredients

- 3 tbsps crushed garlic
- 1 egg yolk
- 2 C. chopped fresh spinach
- 2 boneless skinless chicken breast halves
- 2 tbsps basil pesto
- 1/3 C. chopped sun-dried tomatoes
- 1/4 C. crumbled herbed feta cheese
- 1 frozen puff pastry sheet, thawed, cut in half

Directions

- Get a bowl, combine: egg yolks and garlic.
- Add in the chicken and stir everything and before placing a

lid on the bowl, and putting everything in the fridge for 5 hrs.
- Coat a casserole dish with nonstick spray and then set your oven to 375 degrees before doing anything else.
- Lay out half of your pastry on a cutting board covered with flour and add half a C. of spinach in the middle.
- Place a piece of chicken on top of the spinach, then some pesto, half of the tomatoes, and half of feta.
- Add the rest of the spinach and wrap the chicken with the pastry.
- Crimp the edges of the pastry with your hands and put the pastry in the casserole dish.
- Continue this process for all of your pieces of chicken.
- Cook everything for 37 mins until the chicken is fully done. Shut the heat to the oven and let the contents cool slightly before serving.
- Enjoy.

Amount per serving (4 total)

Timing Information:

Preparation	4 h 15 m
Cooking	35 m
Total Time	4 h 50 m

Nutritional Information:

Calories	515 kcal
Fat	32.6 g
Carbohydrates	33.6g
Protein	22.4 g
Cholesterol	101 mg
Sodium	524 mg

* Percent Daily Values are based on a 2,000 calorie diet.

Souvlaki IV

Ingredients

- 1/4 C. olive oil
- 2 tbsps lemon juice
- 2 cloves garlic, minced
- 1 tsp dried oregano
- 1/2 tsp salt
- 1 1/2 lbs skinless, boneless chicken breast halves - cut into bite-sized pieces
- Sauce:
- 1 (6 oz.) container plain Greek-style yogurt
- 1/2 cucumber - peeled, seeded, and grated
- 1 tbsp olive oil
- 2 tsps white vinegar
- 1 clove garlic, minced
- 1 pinch salt
- 6 wooden skewers, or as needed

Directions

- Take your skewers and submerge them in water before doing anything else.
- Get a bowl, mix: half tsp salt, quarter of a C. of olive oil, chicken, oregano, lemon juice, and 2 cloves of garlic.
- Place a covering on the bowl and put it all in the fridge for 3 hrs.
- Get a 2nd bowl, combine: some salt, yogurt, 1 piece of garlic, 1 tbsp of olive oil, and the cucumbers.
- Place this in the fridge for 3 hrs as well.
- Stake your chicken on the skewers and then grill them for 9 mins, turn them over and cook for 8 more mins.
- Top the chicken with the white sauce.
- Enjoy.

Amount per serving (6 total)

Timing Information:

Preparation	15 m
Cooking	15 m
Total Time	2 h 30 m

Nutritional Information:

Calories	268 kcal
Fat	16.8 g
Carbohydrates	2.6g
Protein	< 25.5 g
Cholesterol	71 mg
Sodium	295 mg

* Percent Daily Values are based on a 2,000 calorie diet.

Greek Style Minty Potato Bake

Ingredients

- 5 lbs potatoes, cut into wedges
- 6 cloves garlic, minced
- 3/4 C. olive oil
- 1 C. water
- 1/4 C. fresh lemon juice
- sea salt to taste
- ground black pepper to taste
- 1 1/2 tbsps dried oregano
- 1 tsp chopped fresh mint
- 1 (8 oz.) package crumbled feta cheese

Directions

- Coat a casserole dish with oil and then set your oven to 450 degrees before doing anything else.
- Get a bowl, mix: pepper, potatoes, salt, garlic, lemon juice,

water, and olive oil. Then layer everything in the dish.
- Cook the contents for 45 mins then top the mix with mint and oregano.
- Add some water (.5 C.) if the potatoes look too dry and cook everything for 42 more mins.
- Now add some feta to the dish before letting the contents sit for 10 mins.
- Enjoy.

Amount per serving (10 total)

Timing Information:

Preparation	20 m
Cooking	1 h 20 m
Total Time	1 h 40 m

Nutritional Information:

Calories	379 kcal
Fat	21.3 g
Carbohydrates	41g
Protein	8 g
Cholesterol	20 mg
Sodium	305 mg

* Percent Daily Values are based on a 2,000 calorie diet.

Easy Greek Dessert

Ingredients

- 3 C. cake flour
- 1 tsp baking soda
- 1/4 tsp salt
- 6 eggs, separated, egg whites in 1 bowl, yolks in another
- 2 C. white sugar
- 1 C. butter, softened
- 2 tsps grated lemon zest
- 2 tbsps lemon juice
- 1 C. plain yogurt

Directions

- Set your oven to 350 degrees before doing anything else.
- Get a tube pan and coat it with oil and then set your oven to 350 degrees before doing anything else.

- Whisk the egg whites until you find them peaking. Then slowly add in sugar (.5 C.) and keep whisking.
- Get a 2nd bowl and whisk the following until airy: lemon juice, cream butter, lemon zest, 1.5 C. sugar, and the yolks.
- Add in the egg whites and fill the tube pan with the mix.
- Cook the contents for 55 mins. Then let the cake sit for 15 mins before slicing it.
- Enjoy.

Amount per serving (14 total)

Timing Information:

Preparation	10 m
Cooking	1 h 20 m
Total Time	1 h 30 m

Nutritional Information:

Calories	380 kcal
Fat	16.1 g
Carbohydrates	53.7g
Protein	6 g
Cholesterol	117 mg
Sodium	264 mg

* Percent Daily Values are based on a 2,000 calorie diet.

Mediterranean Dijon Shrimp Salad

Ingredients

Dijon Vinaigrette:

- 1/4 C. rice wine vinegar
- 2 tbsps Dijon mustard
- 1 large clove garlic, minced
- Big pinch of salt
- Black pepper, to taste
- 2/3 C. extra-virgin olive oil

Pasta Salad:

- 2 medium zucchini, thinly sliced lengthwise
- 1 medium yellow pepper, halved lengthwise, seeded
- 2 tbsps olive oil
- Ground black pepper and salt, to taste

- 1 gallon water
- 2 tbsps salt
- 1 lb. medium pasta shells
- 1 lb. cooked shrimp, halved lengthwise
- 8 oz. cherry tomatoes, halved
- 3/4 C. coarsely chopped, pitted Kalamata olives
- 1 C. crumbled feta cheese
- 1/2 small red onion, cut into small dice
- 2 tsps dried oregano

Directions

- Combine the following in a jar, then shake: pepper, wine vinegar, salt, mustard, and garlic.
- Coat your bell pepper and zucchini with olive oil (2 tbsps), pepper, and salt, then cook them under the broiler for 6 mins then flip them and broil for 5 more mins.

- Place them in a bowl after dicing them.
- Boil your pasta in water and salt for 9 mins then remove all the liquids.
- Now mix the pasta, veggies, and dressing together in a bowl and stir the mix.
- Enjoy.

Amount per serving (6 total)

Timing Information:

Preparation	35 m
Cooking	17 m
Total Time	1 h 22 m

Nutritional Information:

Calories	802 kcal
Fat	45.7 g
Carbohydrates	65.8g
Protein	33.6 g
Cholesterol	185 mg
Sodium	3398 mg

* Percent Daily Values are based on a 2,000 calorie diet.

Greek Couscous

Ingredients

- 3 (6 oz.) packages garlic and herb couscous mix (or any flavor you prefer)
- 1 pint cherry tomatoes, cut in half
- 1 (5 oz.) jar pitted kalamata olives, halved
- 1 C. mixed bell peppers (green, red, yellow, orange), diced
- 1 cucumber, sliced and then halved
- 1/2 C. parsley, finely chopped
- 1 (8 oz.) package crumbled feta cheese
- 1/2 C. Greek vinaigrette salad dressing

Directions

- Get your couscous boiling in water for 5 mins then place a lid

on the pot, and let the grains sit in the water for 17 mins until all the liquid has been absorbed.
- Add the couscous to a bowl with: feta, tomatoes, parsley, olives, cucumbers, and bell peppers.
- Add in the dressing and stir the mix to evenly distribute the oils.
- Enjoy.

Amount per serving (20 total)

Timing Information:

Preparation	30 m
Cooking	15 m
Total Time	45 m

Nutritional Information:

Calories	159 kcal
Fat	6.5 g
Carbohydrates	21.4g
Protein	5.7 g
Cholesterol	10 mg
Sodium	642 mg

* Percent Daily Values are based on a 2,000 calorie diet.

Greek Beans

Ingredients

- 3/4 C. olive oil
- 2 C. chopped onions
- 1 clove garlic, minced
- 2 lbs fresh green beans, rinsed and trimmed
- 3 large tomatoes, diced
- 2 tsps sugar
- salt to taste

Directions

- Stir fry your garlic and onions in olive oil until soft.
- Then add in the salt, beans, sugar, and the tomatoes.
- Set the heat to a lower level and cook everything for 50 more mins until tender.
- Enjoy.

Amount per serving (8 total)

Timing Information:

Preparation	20 m
Cooking	55 m
Total Time	1 h 15 m

Nutritional Information:

Calories	243 kcal
Fat	20.6 g
Carbohydrates	14.6g
Protein	3 g
Cholesterol	0 mg
Sodium	12 mg

* Percent Daily Values are based on a 2,000 calorie diet.

Mediterranean Pork

Ingredients

- 1 lb. pork tenderloin medallions, flatten with a mallet to a thickness of 1/4"
- 1/4 C. all-purpose flour
- 1/2 tsp salt
- 1/4 tsp pepper
- 1 tbsp olive oil
- 1 tbsp chopped fresh rosemary
- 1 clove garlic, minced
- 1/2 C. dry red wine
- 1/2 C. chicken stock
- 1/8 C. sliced kalamata olives
- 1 tbsp minced lemon zest

Directions

- Coat your meat with a mix of pepper, salt, and flour then sear the outsides in olive oil.

- Now cook the meat until it is fully done.
- Remove the meat from the pan and then add in the garlic and rosemary as well as the wine.
- Get everything boiling and continue cooking the contents until they become sauce like then add in the stock and get it all boiling again.
- Continue boiling the mix until half of it has evaporated.
- Finally add in the zest and the olives and cook everything for 1 more min.
- Top your pork with the sauce.
- Enjoy.

Amount per serving (4 total)

Timing Information:

Preparation	20 m
Cooking	15 m
Total Time	35 m

Nutritional Information:

Calories	233 kcal
Fat	10.1 g
Carbohydrates	7.8g
Protein	21.1 g
Cholesterol	63 mg
Sodium	404 mg

* Percent Daily Values are based on a 2,000 calorie diet.

Greek Party Dip

Ingredients

- 1 C. crumbled feta cheese
- 1/2 C. sour cream
- 1/2 C. plain yogurt
- 2 cloves garlic, peeled
- 1/4 tsp salt
- 1/4 tsp freshly ground black pepper

Directions

- Blend the following until smooth: garlic, feta, yogurt, and sour cream.
- Top the mix with some pepper and salt and place it in a jar for later.
- Enjoy with toasted pita pieces.

Amount per serving (8 total)

Timing Information:

Preparation	
Cooking	5 m
Total Time	5 m

Nutritional Information:

Calories	125 kcal
Fat	10 g
Carbohydrates	3.3g
Protein	5.8 g
Cholesterol	35 mg
Sodium	443 mg

* Percent Daily Values are based on a 2,000 calorie diet.

Easy Greek Penne and Steak

Ingredients

- 8 oz. whole wheat penne pasta
- 2 tbsps extra virgin olive oil
- 1 tbsp butter
- 1 (1 lb.) beef rib eye steak
- 1 tbsp butter
- 1 tsp minced garlic
- 1/4 C. chopped shallots
- 1 tbsp soy sauce
- 1/2 C. sun-dried tomato pesto
- 1/2 C. sliced black olives
- 1 C. chopped fresh spinach
- 1 tsp basil
- 1 tbsp chopped parsley
- 1/2 C. crumbled feta cheese
- 3 tbsps sunflower kernels

Directions

- Boil your pasta in water and salt for 9 mins then remove all the liquids.
- Place the pasta in a bowl and coat the noodles with some olive oil.
- Brown your steak in some butter for 9 mins. Then cut the steak into pieces.
- Add in more butter and stir fry your shallots and garlic in it.
- Cook this for 2 mins then add the steak back in and cook the mix for 6 more mins.
- Add in the soy sauce and cook for 1 more min.
- Shut the heat and combine in: sunflower kernels, pesto, feta, olive, parsley, basil, and spinach.
- Add in the pasta to the pan and toss everything.
- Enjoy.

Amount per serving (4 total)

Timing Information:

Preparation	15 m
Cooking	20 m
Total Time	35 m

Nutritional Information:

Calories	579 kcal
Fat	35 g
Carbohydrates	44.7g
Protein	24.5 g
Cholesterol	73 mg
Sodium	710 mg

* Percent Daily Values are based on a 2,000 calorie diet.

Rustic Potatoes with Oregano and Olives

Ingredients

- 2 1/2 lbs potatoes, peeled and cubed
- 1/3 C. olive oil
- 2 cloves garlic, minced
- 3/4 C. whole, pitted kalamata olives
- 1 1/3 C. chopped tomatoes
- 1 tsp dried oregano
- salt and pepper to taste

Directions

- Stir fry your garlic, olives, and potatoes for 7 mins then add in the oregano and tomatoes.
- Place a lid on the pot and gently boil everything for 35 mins until the veggies are soft.

- Simmer the contents with a low heat and once the potatoes are done top everything with some pepper and salt.
- Enjoy.

Amount per serving (6 total)

Timing Information:

Preparation	25 m
Cooking	30 m
Total Time	55 m

Nutritional Information:

Calories	309 kcal
Fat	16.7 g
Carbohydrates	36.7g
Protein	4.5 g
Cholesterol	0 mg
Sodium	289 mg

* Percent Daily Values are based on a 2,000 calorie diet.

Greek Honey Cake Dessert II

Ingredients

- 1 C. all-purpose flour
- 1 1/2 tsps baking powder
- 1/4 tsp salt
- 1/2 tsp ground cinnamon
- 1 tsp orange zest
- 3/4 C. butter
- 3/4 C. white sugar
- 3 eggs
- 1/4 C. milk
- 1 C. chopped walnuts
- 1 C. white sugar
- 1 C. honey
- 3/4 C. water
- 1 tsp lemon juice

Directions

- Coat a square pan with oil and then set your oven to 350 degrees before doing anything else.
- Get a bowl, mix: orange rind, flour, cinnamon, baking powder, and salt.
- Get a 2nd bowl, and whisk, until airy: 3/4 C. sugar, and butter.
- Gradually add in your eggs and continuing whisking. Once all the eggs have been beaten add the flour mix and the milk and continue whisking.
- Finally add the nuts and stir the mix once more before entering everything into your pan and cooking it for 45 mins in the oven.
- At the same time, get the following boiling, then simmer it, over low heat, for 7 mins: water, 1 C. sugar, and honey.
- Add the lemon juice and simmer for 3 more mins.
- Let your cake cool for 15 mins before topping with the honey sauce.

- Enjoy.

Amount per serving (12 total)

Timing Information:

Preparation	30 m
Cooking	40 m
Total Time	1 h 10 m

Nutritional Information:

Calories	423 kcal
Fat	19.3 g
Carbohydrates	62.3g
Protein	4.5 g
Cholesterol	77 mg
Sodium	196 mg

* Percent Daily Values are based on a 2,000 calorie diet.

Veggie Salad

Ingredients

- 1 red bell pepper, cut into 1/2 inch pieces
- 1 yellow bell pepper, chopped
- 1 medium eggplant, cubed
- 3 small yellow squash, cut in 1/4 inch slices
- 6 tbsps extra virgin olive oil
- 1/4 tsp salt
- 1/4 tsp ground black pepper
- 1 1/2 oz. sun-dried tomatoes, soaked in 1/2 C. boiling water
- 1/2 C. torn arugula leaves
- 1/2 C. chopped fresh basil
- 2 tbsps balsamic vinegar
- 2 tbsps minced garlic
- 4 oz. crumbled feta cheese
- 1 (12 oz.) package farfalle pasta

Directions

- Cover a casserole dish with foil and nonstick spray. Then set your oven to 450 degrees before doing anything else.
- Get a bowl, combine: pepper, bell peppers, salt, eggplants, olive oil (2 tbsps), and squash.
- Layer everything in your casserole dish.
- Cook everything in the oven for 27 mins and stir the contents half way.
- Boil your pasta in water and salt for 11 mins then remove all the liquid.
- Place the pasta in a bowl, with: basil, liquid from the tomatoes, pepper, veggies, salt, arugula, feta, pasta, garlic, sun dried tomatoes balsamic, and olive oil.
- Place the mix in the fridge for 60 mins then serve.
- Enjoy.

Amount per serving (6 total)

Timing Information:

Preparation	20 m
Cooking	40 m
Total Time	1 h

Nutritional Information:

Calories	446 kcal
Fat	19.5 g
Carbohydrates	56.9g
Protein	13.8 g
Cholesterol	17 mg
Sodium	324 mg

* Percent Daily Values are based on a 2,000 calorie diet.

Greek Grilled Cheese

Ingredients

- 1 1/2 tsps butter, softened
- 2 slices whole wheat bread, or your favorite bread
- 2 tbsps crumbled feta cheese
- 2 slices Cheddar cheese
- 1 tbsp chopped red onion
- 1/4 tomato, thinly sliced

Directions

- Coat one side of each piece of bread with some butter then layer the following on one piece: tomato, feta, red onions, and cheddar.
- Place the other piece of bread on top to form a sandwich and make sure the buttered side is facing outwards.

- Fry your sandwich for 3 mins on one side and 2 mins on the other.
- Enjoy.

Amount per serving (1 total)

Timing Information:

Preparation	5 m
Cooking	5 m
Total Time	10 m

Nutritional Information:

Calories	482 kcal
Fat	30.9 g
Carbohydrates	27.1g
Protein	24.6 g
Cholesterol	92 mg
Sodium	876 mg

* Percent Daily Values are based on a 2,000 calorie diet.

Avgolemono Chicken Stew

Ingredients

- 1 (3 lb.) whole chicken
- 1/2 C. uncooked white rice
- salt and freshly ground black pepper to taste
- 3 egg, beaten
- 2 lemons, juiced

Directions

- Clean you chicken and remove the insides if needed.
- Get the chicken boiling, submerged in water.
- Once the contents are boiling place a lid on the pan, set the heat to low, and cook the mix for 55 mins.
- Skim the top of the liquid occasionally as the chicken cooks.

- Remove the chicken from the pan and shred it when it is cool enough to handle.
- Keep the water boiling and then add in pepper, salt, and rice.
- Cook the rice with a low level of heat for 25 more mins.
- Get a bowl and mix the lemon juice and eggs.
- Grab a ladle and add some broth to the bowl with your eggs.
- Keep adding broth until the eggs are hot. Then add the eggs to the big pot.
- Add a bit more pepper and salt to the mix as well as the chicken.
- Enjoy.

Amount per serving (6 total)

Timing Information:

Preparation	15 m
Cooking	1 h
Total Time	1 h 15 m

Nutritional Information:

Calories	321 kcal
Fat	17.4 g
Carbohydrates	16.4g
Protein	25.6 g
Cholesterol	154 mg
Sodium	94 mg

* Percent Daily Values are based on a 2,000 calorie diet.

Souvlaki V

Ingredients

- 2 lbs lamb, cut into 1 inch square cubes
- 1/2 C. olive oil
- 1 C. red wine
- 1 tsp salt
- freshly ground black pepper to taste
- 1 tsp dried oregano
- 1 tbsp dried mint, crushed
- 1 clove garlic, chopped
- 4 C. plain yogurt
- 1 cucumber, shredded
- 4 cloves garlic, minced
- 2 tbsps olive oil
- 1/2 tsp dried dill weed
- salt and pepper to taste
- 8 pita bread rounds
- 2 tbsps olive oil
- 1 red onion, thinly sliced
- 1 tomato, thinly sliced

Directions

- Get a bowl, combine the following: garlic, mint, lamb, oregano, half a C. of olive oil, pepper, red wine, and one tsp salt.
- Stir the contents and place a covering on everything and put it all in the fridge for 4 hours.
- Get a 2nd bowl, mix: minced garlic, yogurt, 2 tbsps olive oil, cucumber, pepper, dill, and salt.
- Place this in the fridge as well.
- Form kebabs from the mix and cook them on the grill for 6 mins then flip each one and cook for 5 more mins.
- Coat each piece of bread with some olive oil and then toast them on the grill.
- Serve these kebabs with a piece of bread, some red onions, and tomatoes.

- Top the meat with the white sauce in the fridge.
- Enjoy.

Amount per serving (8 total)

Timing Information:

Preparation	30 m
Cooking	20 m
Total Time	1 d 50 m

Nutritional Information:

Calories	814 kcal
Fat	53.2 g
Carbohydrates	46.5g
Protein	31.1 g
Cholesterol	91 mg
Sodium	766 mg

* Percent Daily Values are based on a 2,000 calorie diet.

Shrimp with Feta and Tomatoes

Ingredients

- 4 tbsps extra virgin olive oil
- 1 medium onion, finely chopped
- 3/4 C. chopped green onion
- 2 cloves garlic, crushed
- 2 C. chopped, peeled tomatoes
- 1/2 C. dry white wine
- 1/4 C. chopped fresh parsley
- 1 tbsp chopped fresh oregano
- salt and pepper to taste
- 2 lbs large uncooked shrimp, peeled
- 4 oz. crumbled feta cheese

Directions

- Stir fry your onions until see through.
- Add in garlic and green onions.
- Cook for 4 more mins.

- Now add in: pepper, tomatoes, salt, wine and parsley.
- Place a cover on the pot and gently boil everything with a low level of heat for 35 mins.
- Now set your oven to 500 degrees before doing anything else.
- Layer half of the sauce into a casserole dish and top everything with the shrimp and add more sauce.
- Add a finally layering of feta over everything.
- Cook the contents in the oven for 13 mins then top with some more parsley.
- Enjoy.

Amount per serving (8 total)

Timing Information:

Preparation	30 m
Cooking	15 m
Total Time	45 m

Nutritional Information:

Calories	218 kcal
Fat	10.9 g
Carbohydrates	5.2g
Protein	21.4 g
Cholesterol	185 mg
Sodium	436 mg

* Percent Daily Values are based on a 2,000 calorie diet.

Thanks for Reading! Now Let's Try some Sushi and Dump Dinners....

Send the Book!

To grab this **box set** simply follow the link mentioned above, or tap the book cover.

This will take you to a page where you can simply enter your email address and a PDF version of the **box set** will be emailed to you.

I hope you are ready for some serious cooking!

[Send the Book!](#)

You will also receive updates about all my new books when they are free.

Also don't forget to like and subscribe on the social networks. I love meeting my readers. Links to all my profiles are below so please click and connect :)

[Facebook](#)

[Twitter](#)

COME ON...
LET'S BE FRIENDS :)

I adore my readers and love connecting with them socially. Please follow the links below so we can connect on Facebook, Twitter, and Google+.

Facebook

Twitter

I also have a blog that I regularly update for my readers so check it out below.

My Blog

Can I Ask A Favour?

If you found this book interesting, or have otherwise found any benefit in it. Then may I ask that you post a review of it on Amazon? Nothing excites me more than new reviews, especially reviews which suggest new topics for writing. I do read all reviews and I always factor feedback into my newer works.

So if you are willing to take ten minutes to write what you sincerely thought about this book then please visit our Amazon page and post your opinions.

Again thank you!

INTERESTED IN OTHER EASY COOKBOOKS?

Everything is easy! Check out my Amazon Author page for more great cookbooks:

For a complete listing of all my books please see my author page.

Made in the USA
Middletown, DE
14 September 2017